Doctor Knock-Knock's Official Knock-Knock Dictionary

by Joseph Rosenbloom
illustrated by Joyce Behr

Sterling Publishing Co., Inc. New York

Books by the Same Author

Bananas Don't Grow on Trees
Biggest Riddle Book in the World
Daffy Dictionary
Doctor Knock-Knock's Official
Knock-Knock Dictionary
Gigantic Joke Book
How Do You Make an Elephant Laugh?
Looniest Limerick Book in the World
Mad Scientist: Riddles, Jokes, Fun
Monster Madness
Polar Bears Like It Hot
Ridiculous Nicholas Pet Riddles
Ridiculous Nicholas Riddle Book
Silly Verse (and Even Worse)
Snappy Put-Downs & Funny Insults

To: Julie and Danielle

387 Park Avenue South, New York, N.Y. 10016
Distributed in Canada by Sterling Publishing
c/o Canadian Manda Group, One Atlantic Avenue, Suite 105
Toronto, Ontario, Canada M6K 3E7
Distributed in Great Britain by Chrysalis Books
64 Brewery Road, London N7 9NT, England
Distributed in Australia by Capricorn Ltd.
P.O. Box 704, Windsor, NSW 2756 Australia
Manufactured in the United States of America

Library of Congress Catalog Card No.: 76-19796
Sterling ISBN 0-8069-4536-2 Trade
4537-0 Library
8936-x Paper

KNOCK-KNOCK

Who's there?
Abyssinia.
Abyssinia who?
Abyssinia behind bars one of these days.

Who's there?
Acid.
Acid who?
Acid down and be quiet!

Who's there?
Adelia.
Adelia who?
Adelia the cards
after you cut the deck.

Who's there?
Adlai.
Adlai who?
Adlai a bet on that.

KNOCK-KNOCK

Who's there?
Adolf.
Adolf who?
Adolf ball hit me in the mowf.

Who's there?
Agatha.
Agatha who?
Agatha headache. Do you have an aspirin?

Who's there?
Aida.
Aida who?
Aida lot of candy and now my stomach aches.

Who's there?
Alda.
Alda who?
Alda time you knew who it was!

Who's there?
Alec.
Alec who?
Alec-tricity. Isn't that a shock?

Who's there?
Alex.
Alex who?
Alex the questions around here.

Who's there?
Alfalfa.
Alfalfa who?
Alfalfa (I'll fall for) you, if you blow in my ear.

Who's there?
Alfie.
Alfie who?
Alfie you in my dreams.

Who's there?
Alfred.
Alfred who?
Alfred the needle if you sew.

Who's there?
Alice.
Alice who?
"I'm Alice chasing rainbows . . ."

Who's there?
Allied.
Allied who?
Allied, so sue me!

Who's there?
Alma.
Alma who?
Alma not going to tell you.

Who's there?
Almond.
Almond who?
Almond the side of the law.

Who's there?
Aloysius. (Pronounced A-loo-ish-us)
Aloysius who?
"Aloysius for Christmas is my two front teeth . . ."

Who's there?
Alpaca.
Alpaca who?
Alpaca the trunk, you pack-a the suitcase.

Who's there?
Amahl.
Amahl who?
Amahl shook up.

Who's there?
Amana.
Amana who?
Amana bad mood!

Who's there?
Amazon.
Amazon who?
Amazon of a gun!

KNOCK-KNOCK

Who's there?
Ammonia.
Ammonia who?
Ammonia little kid.

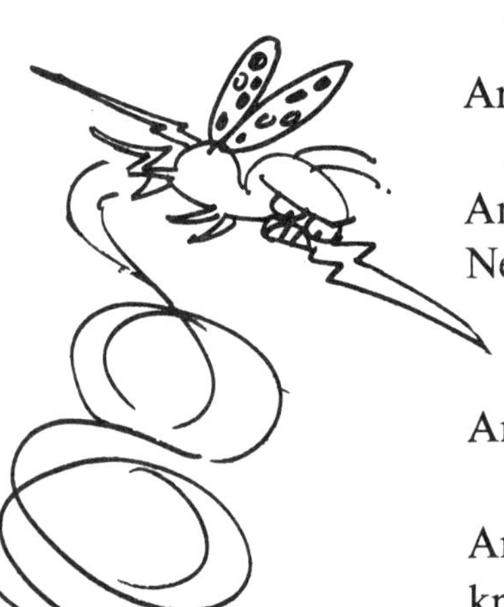

Who's there?
Amory.
Amory who?
Amory Christmas and a happy New Year!

Who's there?
Amsterdam.
Amsterdam who?
Amsterdam tired of all these knock-knock jokes.

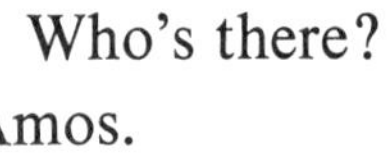

Who's there?
Amos.
Amos who?
Amos-quito bit me.
Knock-knock.
Who's there?
Andy.
Andy who?
Andy bit me again.

Who's there?
Analyze.
Analyze who?
"My analyze over the ocean, my analyze over the sea . . ."

Knock-Knock.
Who's there?
Anatomy.
Anatomy who?
"Oh, bring back my anatomy . . ."

Who's there?
Anita.
Anita who?
Anita you like I need a hole in the head.

Who's there?
Anna.
Anna who?
Anna going to tell you.

Who's there?
Anne Boleyn.
Anne Boleyn who?
Anne Boleyn alley.

KNOCK-KNOCK

Who's there?
Annetta.
Annetta who?
Annetta wisecrack and you're off the bus!

Who's there?
Anthem.
Anthem who?
You anthem devil, you!

Who's there?
Arch.
Arch who?
You catching cold?

Who's there?
Argo.
Argo who?
Argo fly a kite!

Who's there?
Aries.
Aries who?
Aries a reason why I talk this way.

Who's there?
Arizona.
Arizona who?
Arizona room for one of us in this neighborhood.

Who's there?
Armageddon.
Armageddon who?
Armageddon out of here!

Who's there?
Armenia.
Armenia who?
Armenia every word I say.

Who's there?
Arnold.
Arnold who?
Arnold (an old) friend from Transylvania.
Knock-Knock.
Who's there?
Samoa.
Samoa who?
Samoa old friends from Transylvania.

KNOCK-KNOCK

Who's there?
Arthur.
Arthur who?
Arthur anymore at home like you?

Who's there?
Ashley.
Ashley who?
Ashley-t's foot (athlete's foot).

Who's there?
Asia.
Asia who?
Asia going to invite me in?

Who's there?
Athena.
Athena who?
Athena flying saucer!

Who's there?
Atlas.
Atlas who?
Atlas it's Friday.

Who's there?
Atomic.
Atomic who?
Atomic ache.

Who's there?
Aunt Lou.
Aunt Lou who?
Aunt Lou do you think you are?

Who's there?
Avenue.
Avenue who?
Avenue heard the good news?

Knock-Knock

B

Who's there?
Banana.
Banana who?
Knock-Knock.
Who's there?
Banana.
Banana who?
Knock-Knock.
Who's there?
Banana.
Banana who?
Knock-Knock.
Who's there?
Orange.
Orange who?
Orange you glad I didn't say banana?

Who's there?
Barbara.
Barbara who?
"Barbara black sheep, have you any wool . . ."

Who's there?
Bella.
Bella who?
Bella bottom trousers.

Who's there?
Bertha.
Bertha who?
Bertha-day greetings.

Who's there?
Beryl.
Beryl who?
Beryl of monkeys.

Who's there?
Betty.
Betty who?
Betty-bye!

KNOCK-KNOCK

Who's there?
Bibi.
Bibi who?
Bibi gun.

Who's there?
Bitter Bianca.
Bitter Bianca who?
Bitter Bianca next stagecoach out of town, pardner.

Who's there?
Bolivia.
Bolivia who?
Bolivia me, I know what I'm talking about.

Who's there?
Boo.
Boo who?
Well, you don't have to cry about it.

Who's there?
Bridget.
Bridget who?
London Bridget.

Who's there?
Brigham.
Brigham who?
"Brigham back my sunshine to me . . ."

Who's there?
Burton.
Burton who?
Burton the hand is worth
two in the bush.

KNOCK-KNOCK

Who's there?
Butch.
Butch who?
Butch your arms around me.
Knock-Knock.
Who's there?
Jimmy.
Jimmy who?
Butch your arms around me; Jimmy a little kiss.
Knock-Knock.
Who's there?
Aldous.
Aldous who?
Butch your arms around me; Jimmy a little kiss or Aldous go home.

Who's there?
Butcher.
Butcher who?
Butcher money where your mouth is.

Who's there?
Button.
Button who?
Button in is not polite.

Who's there?
Candy.
Candy who?
Candy cow jump over the moon?

Who's there?
Cantaloupe.
Cantaloupe who?
Cantaloupe today.
Knock-Knock.
Who's there?
Lettuce.
Lettuce who?
Lettuce try tomorrow.

Who's there?
Carmen.
Carmen who?
Carmen get it!

Who's there?
Cash.
Cash who?
I knew you were some kind of nut.

Who's there?
Cecil.
Cecil who?
"Cecil have music wherever she goes . . ."

Who's there?
Celeste.
Celeste who?
Celeste time I'm going to tell you this.

Who's there?
Cello.
Cello who?
Cello dere!

Who's there?
Cereal.
Cereal who?
Cereal pleasure to meet you.

Who's there?
Cheese.
Cheese who?
Cheese a cute girl.

Who's there?
Chester.
Chester who?
"Chester song at twilight . . ."

Who's there?
Chesterfield.
Chesterfield who?
Chesterfield my leg, so I slapped him.

Who's there?
Cigarette.
Cigarette who?
Cigarette (it's a great) life if you don't weaken.

Who's there?
Colleen.
Colleen who?
Colleen all cars!

KNOCK-KNOCK

Who's there?
Collier.
Collier who?
Collier big brother.
See if I care!

Who's there?
Cologne. (Pronounced Co-lone)
Cologne who?
Cologne me names won't help.

Who's there?
Congo.
Congo who?
Congo on meeting like this.

Who's there?
Cook.
Cook who?
Cuckoo yourself. I didn't come here to be insulted.

Who's there?
Cozy.
Cozy who?
Cozy who's knocking.

Who's there?
Custer.
Custer who?
Custer a penny to find out.

Who's there?
Cynthia.
Cynthia who?
Cynthia been away, I've been so sad.

knock-knock

D

Who's there?
Daisy.
Daisy who?
Daisy plays, nights he sleeps.

Who's there?
Dana.
Dana who?
Dana talk with your mouth full.

Who's there?
Darius.
Darius who?
Darius a lot I have to tell you.

Who's there?
Darren.
Darren who?
Darren young man on the flying trapeze.

Who's there?
Darwin.
Darwin who?
I'll be Darwin (there when) you open the door.

Who's there?
Daryl.
Daryl who?
"Daryl never ever be another you . . ."

Who's there?
Datsun.
Datsun who?
Datsun old joke.

Who's there?
Dawn.
Dawn who?
Dawn do anything I wouldn't do.

Knock-Knock

Who's there?
Deanna.
Deanna who?
Deanna-mals are restless—open the cage!

Who's there?
Deduct.
Deduct who?
Donald Deduct.

Who's there?
Deena.
Deena who?
Deena hear me the first time?

Who's there?
Delores.
Delores who?
Delores on the side of the good guys.

Who's there?
Denis.
Denis who?
Denis anyone?

Who's there?
Dennis.
Dennis who?
Dennis says I've got a cavity.

Who's there?
Denver.
Denver who?
Denver the good old days.

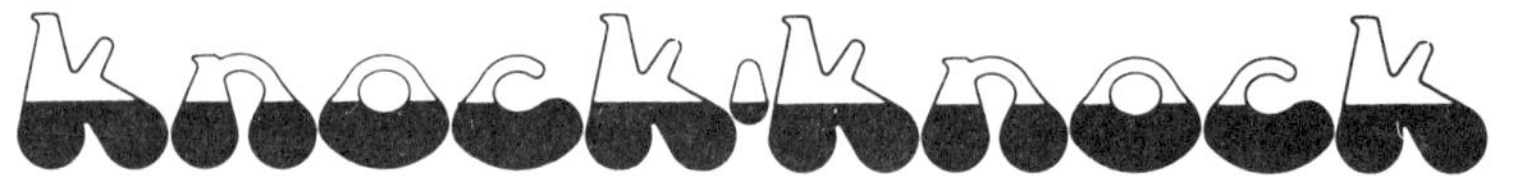

Who's there?
Desiree. (Pronounced Dez-ee-ray)
Desiree who?
Desiree (There's a ray) of sunshine in my life.

Who's there?
Detail.
Detail who?
Detail-a phone operator.

Who's there?
Dewey.
Dewey who?
Dewey have to keep telling knock-knock jokes?

Who's there?
DeWitt.
DeWitt who?
DeWitt (do it) now or never.

Who's there?
Diesel.
Diesel who?
Diesel teach me to go around knocking on doors.

Who's there?
Dinah.
Dinah who?
Dinah shoot until you see the whites of their eyes.

Who's there?
Dino.
Dino who?
Dino the answer.
Knock-Knock.
Who's there?
Alaska.
Alaska who?
Alaska my mommy.

KNOCK-KNOCK

Who's there?
Diploma.
Diploma who?
Diploma to fix the leak.

Who's there?
Disaster.
Disaster who?
Disaster be my lucky day!

Who's there?
Disguise.
Disguise who?
Disguise (the sky's) the limit.

Who's there?
Dishes.
Dishes who?
Dishes the end of the road.

Who's there?
Disk.
Disk who?
Disk is a recorded message.

Who's there?

Dmitri.

Dmitri who?

Dmitri is where the lamb chops grow.

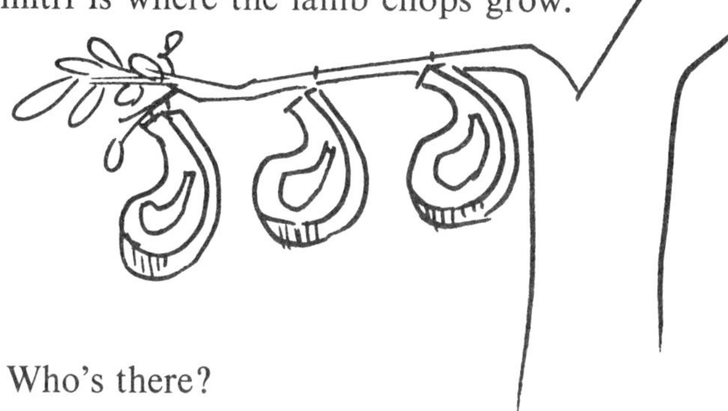

Who's there?

Don Giovanni.

Don Giovanni who?

Don Giovanni (don't you want to) talk to me?

Who's there?

Don Juan.

Don Juan who?

Don Juan to go to school today.

Who's there?

Donald.

Donald who?

"Donald come baby, cradle and all . . ."

Who's there?

Donalette.

Donalette who?

Donalette the bed bugs bite.

knock-knock

Who's there?
Donna.
Donna who?
"Donna sit under the apple tree
with anyone else but me . . ."

Who's there?
Donna Mae.
Donna Mae who?
Donna Mae-k you an offer you can't refuse.

Who's there?
Doris.
Doris who?
Doris slammed on my finger. Help!

Who's there?
Dotty.
Dotty who?
Dotty way the cookie crumbles.

Who's there?
Doughnut.
Doughnut who?
Doughnut open until Christmas.

Who's there?
Dozen.
Dozen who?
Dozen anyone answer the door?

Who's there?
Dragon.
Dragon who?
Dragon your feet again?

Who's there?
Drucilla.
Drucilla who?
Drucilla (you silly) kid, you!

Knock-Knock

Who's there?
Duane.
Duane who?
Duane the bathtub, I'm dwowning.

Who's there?
Dummy.
Dummy who?
Dummy a favor and get lost.

Who's there?
Dunce.
Dunce who?
Dunce-ay another word.

Who's there?
Dustin Hoffman.
Dustin Hoffman who?
Dustin Hoffman (dustin' off my) welcome mat for you.

Who's there?
Dwayne.
Dwayne who?
"Dwayne in Spain falls mainly on the plain . . ."

Who's there?
Dwight.
Dwight who?
Dwight way and the wrong way.

KNOCK-KNOCK

E

Who's there?
Earl.
Earl who?
Earl be glad to tell you if you open the door.

Who's there?
Ears.
Ears who?
Ears looking at you!

Who's there?
Eddie.
Eddie who?
Eddie body home?

Who's there?
Egypt.
Egypt who?
Egypt you when he sold you that busted doorbell.

Who's there?
Elke.
Elke who?
"Elke seltzer . . .
Plop, plop, fizz, fizz . . ."

Who's there?
Ella.
Ella who?
Ella-vator. Doesn't that give you a lift?

Who's there?
Ella Mann.
Ella Mann who?
Ella Mann-tary, my dear Watson.

Who's there?
Ellen.
Ellen who?
Ellen-eed is love.

Who's there?
Elsie.
Elsie who?
Elsie you around.

Who's there?
Emma.
Emma who?
Emma glad you asked that.

Who's there?
Emmett.
Emmett who?
Emmett your service.

Who's there?
Enoch.
Enoch who?
Enoch and Enoch but nobody opens the door.

Who's there?
Esther.
Esther who?
Esther anything I can do for you?

Who's there?
Ether.
Ether who?
Ether Bunny.
Knock-Knock.
Who's there?
Cargo.
Cargo who?
Cargo "beep-beep" and run
over Ether Bunny.
Knock-Knock.
Who's there?
Stella.
Stella who?
Stella 'nother Ether Bunny.
Knock-Knock.
Who's there?
Consumption.
Consumption who?
Consumption be done about
all these Ether Bunnies?

KNOCK-KNOCK

Who's there?
Eugenie.
Eugenie who?
Eugenie from the bottle who will grant you three wishes.

Knock-Knock.
Who's there?
Hugh.
Hugh who?
Hugh let me out of this bottle!

Who's there?
Euripedes. (Pronounced You-rippa-deez)
Euripedes who?
Euripedes pants and I'll sue you.

Knock-Knock.
Who's there?
Eumenides. (Pronounced You-menny-deez)
Eumenides who?
Eumenides and I won't.

Who's there?
Europe.
Europe who?
Europe to no good.

Who's there?
Eustace.
Eustace who?
Come Eustace (just as) you are.

Who's there?
Eva.
Eva who?
Eva I told you, would you let me in?

Who's there?
Eyesore.
Eyesore who?
Eyesore (I sure) do like you.

Who's there?
Ezra.
Ezra who?
Ezra no hope for me?

KNOCK-KNOCK

F

Who's there?
Fanny.
Fanny who?
Fanny-body home?

Who's there?
Farley.
Farley who?
Farley the leader.

Who's there?
Fatso.
Fatso who?
Fatso matter with you?

Who's there?
Felix.
Felix who?
Felix-cited all over.

Who's there?
Ferdie.
Ferdie who?
Ferdie last time, open the door!

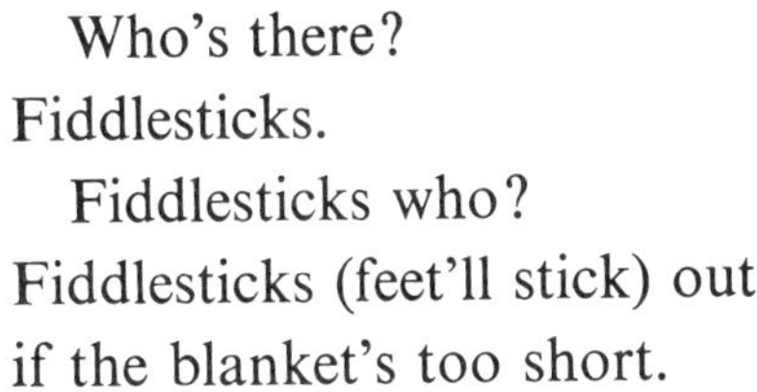

Who's there?
Fiddlesticks.
Fiddlesticks who?
Fiddlesticks (feet'll stick) out if the blanket's too short.

Who's there?
Fiona. (Pronounced Fee-oh-na)
Fiona who?
Fiona had something better to do, do you think we'd hang around here?

Who's there?
Fletcher.
Fletcher who?
Fletcher self go!

KNOCK-KNOCK

Who's there?
Franz.
Franz who?
"Franz, Romans, countrymen . . ."

Who's there?
Freddie.
Freddie who?
Freddie or not, here I come.

Who's there?
Freighter.
Freighter who?
Freighter open the door?

Who's there?
Fresno.
Fresno who?
"Rudolf the Fresno reindeer . . ."

Who's there?
Genoa.
Genoa who?
Genoa new knock-knock joke?

Who's there?
Gerald.
Gerald who?
Gerald washed up, kid.

Who's there?
Gilda.
Gilda who?
Gilda umpire!

Who's there?
Gino.
Gino who?
Gino (you know) me, open the door.

Knock-Knock

Who's there?
Gladys.
Gladys who?
Gladys see you.

Who's there?
Gopher.
Gopher who?
Gopher (go for) broke.

Who's there?
Gordie.
Gordie who?
Gordie-rectly to jail. Do not pass Go. Do not collect $200.

Who's there?
Gorilla.
Gorilla who?
Gorilla cheese sandwich.

Who's there?
Grammar.
Grammar who?
Grammar crackers. Pretty crummy, huh?

Who's there?
Greta.
Greta who?
You Greta my nerves.

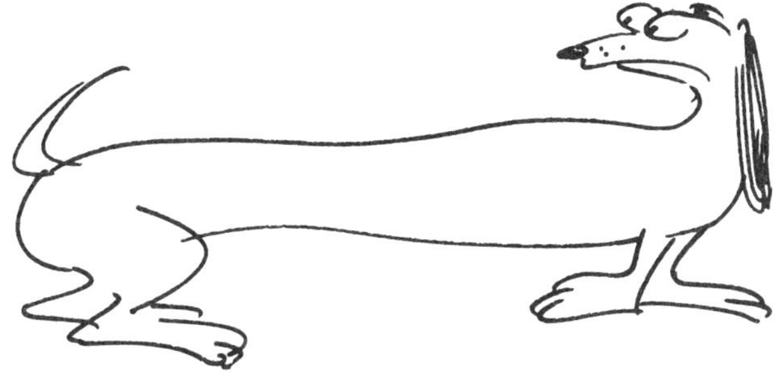

Who's there?
Gretel.
Gretel who?
"Gretel-long little dogie . . ."

Who's there?
Guinevere.
Guinevere who?
Guinevere going to get together?

Who's there?
Guthrie.
Guthrie who?
Guthrie blind mice.

KNOCK-KNOCK

H

Who's there?
Hacienda.
Hacienda who?
Hacienda (that's the end of) the story.

Who's there?
Hagar.
Hagar who?
"Hagar, you with the stars in your eyes . . ."

Who's there?
Hair.
Hair who?
Hair today, gone tomorrow.

Who's there?
Handsome.
Handsome who?
Handsome pretzel sticks through the keyhole and I'll tell you more.

Who's there?
Hannah.
Hannah who?
"Hannah partridge in a pear tree . . ."

Who's there?
Hanover.
Hanover who?
Hanover your money.

Who's there?
Hardy.
Hardy who?
Hardy har, har!

Who's there?
Harmon.
Harmon who?
Harmon your side.

Who's there?
Harold.
Harold who?
Harold are you?

KNOCK-KNOCK

Who's there?
Havana.
Havana who?
Havana wonderful time, wish you were here.

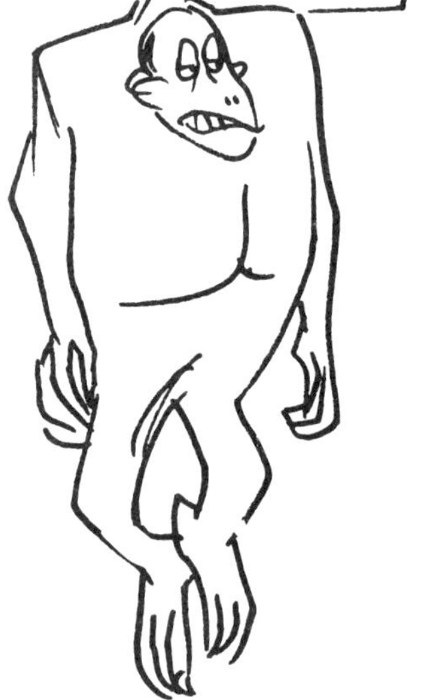

Who's there?
Hawaii.
Hawaii who?
Fine, until you showed up.

Who's there?
Haydn. (Pronounced High-din)
Haydn who?
Haydn (hidin') in this closet is a bore!

Who's there?
Heart.
Heart who?
Heart who hear you, talk louder.

Who's there?
Heaven.
Heaven who?
Heaven seen you for a long time.

Who's there?
Heide.
Heide who?
Heide-clare war on you!

Who's there?
Heifer.
Heifer who?
Heifer (half a) cow is better than none.

Who's there?
Hiawatha.
Hiawatha who?
Hiawatha very bad today.

Who's there?
Hiram.
Hiram who?
Hiram fine, how are you?

KNOCK-KNOCK

Who's there?
Hoffman.
Hoffman who?
I'll Hoffman I'll puff, and I'll blow your house down.

Who's there?
Hollis.
Hollis who?
Hollis forgiven. Come home.

Who's there?
Homer.
Homer who?
Homer-gain.

Who's there?
Hominy.
Hominy who?
Hominy times are we going through this?

Who's there?
Honda.
Honda who?
"Honda the spreading chestnut tree . . ."

Who's there?
Hot air.
Hot air who?
Hot air (hi-dere) pardner! How ya doin'?

Who's there?
Houseboy.
Houseboy who?
Great! Houseboy (how's by) you?

Who's there?
Howard Hughes.
Howard Hughes who?
Howard Hughes like a punch in the nose?

Who's there?
Howell.
Howell who?
Howell you have your pizza, plain or with sausage?

Who's therc?
Howie.
Howie who?
I'm okay, how are you?

Who's there?
Hubie.
Hubie who?
Hubie-ginning to see the light?

Who's there?
Hugo.
Hugo who?
Hugo your way and I'll go my way.

Who's there?
Hyman.
Hyman who?
"Hyman the mood for love . . ."

Who's there?
Ice cream soda.
Ice cream soda who?
Ice cream soda (I scream so the) whole world will know what a nut you are.

Who's there?
Ichabod.
Ichabod who?
Ichabod (it's a bad) night out. Can I borrow your umbrella?

Who's there?
Ida.
Ida who?
Idaho—not Ida-who! Can't you spell?

Who's there?
Igloo.
Igloo who?
"Igloo knew Suzie like I know Suzie . . ."

Who's there?
Iguana.
Iguana who?
"Iguana hold your hand . . ."

Who's there?
Ike.
Ike who?
Ike-n't stop laughing.

Who's there?
Ilka.
Ilka who?
Ilka-pone (Al Capone).

Who's there?
Ilona.
Ilona who?
Ilona Ranger.

Who's there?
Ina Claire.
Ina Claire who?
"Ina Claire day, you can see forever . . ."

Who's there?
India.
India who?
"India good old summertime . . ."

Who's there?
Indonesia.
Indonesia who?
I look at you and I get weak Indonesia.

Who's there?
Iona.
Iona who?
"Iona have one life to give for my country . . ."

Who's there?
Iris.
Iris who?
Iris you were here.

KNOCK-KNOCK

Who's there?
Irma.
Irma who?
Irma big girl now.

Who's there?
Isabella.
Isabella who?
Isabella out of order?

Who's there?
Isadore.
Isadore who?
Isadore locked? I can't get in.

Who's there?
Isaiah.
Isaiah who?
Isaiah nothing till you open the door.

Who's there?
Ivan.
Ivan who?
Ivan my mommy!

Who's there?
Ivory.
Ivory who?
Ivory strong like Tarzan.
Knock-Knock.
Who's there?
Audacity.
Audacity who?
Audacity (oh, that is the) way to be.

Who's there?
Izzy.
Izzy who?
Izzy come, Izzy go.

KNOCK-KNOCK

J

Who's there?
Jaguar.
Jaguar who?
Jaguar nimble, Jaguar quick.

Who's there?
Jamaica.
Jamaica who?
Jamaica mistake?

Who's there?
Jaws.
Jaws who?
Jaws truly.

Who's there?
Jerrold.
Jerrold who?
Jerrold friend, that's who!

Who's there?
Jess.
Jess who?
Jess one of those things.

Who's there?
Jessica.
Jessica who?
Jessica (you're sicker) than I thought.

Who's there?
Jester.
Jester who?
Jester minute, pardner.

Who's there?
Jethro.
Jethro who?
Jethro the boat and stop talking so much.

Who's there?
Jewel.
Jewel who?
Jewel (you'll) remember me after you see my face.

Knock-Knock

Who's there?
Joan.
Joan who?
Joan call us, we'll call you.

Who's there?
Joanne.
Joanne who?
Joanne (show and) tell.

Who's there?
Joe Namath.
Joe Namath who?
Joe Namath (your name is) not on the door. That's why I knocked.

Knock-Knock.
Who's there?
Amy Namath.
Amy Namath who?
"Amy Namath (A my name is) Alice and my husband's name is Allan . . ."

Who's there?
John.
John who?
John the Navy.
Knock-Knock.
Who's there?
Cedar.
Cedar who?
John the Navy and Cedar world.

Who's there?
José.
José who?
"José can you see . . ."

Who's there?
Josette.
Josette who?
Josette down.

Who's there?
Juan.
Juan who?
Juan of these days, pow, right in the kisser!

KNOCK-KNOCK

Who's there?
Juanita.
Juanita who?
Juanita (want to eat a) 'nother hot dog?

Who's there?
Juicy.
Juicy who?
Juicy what I just saw?

Who's there?
Juno.
Juno who?
Juno what time it is?

Who's there?
Jupiter.
Jupiter who?
Jupiter fly in my soup?

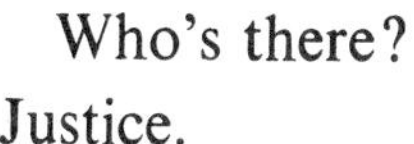

Who's there?
Justice.
Justice who?
Justice I thought.
No one's home.

Who's there?
Justin.
Justin who?
Justin time for a knuckle sandwich.

KNOCK-KNOCK

K

Who's there?
Kaye.
Kaye who?
Kaye será será.

Who's there?
Kenneth.
Kenneth who?
Kenneth little kids play with you?

Who's there?
Kent.
Kent who?
Kent you tell who it is?

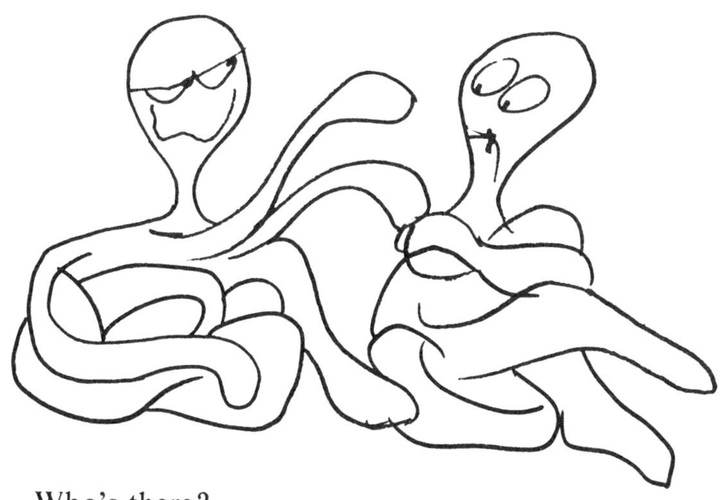

Who's there?
Kipper.
Kipper who?
Kipper hands to yourself.

Who's there?
Kurt and Conan.
Kurt and Conan who?
Kurt and Conan (curtain coming) down on the last act.

KNOCK-KNOCK

L

Who's there?
Lauren.
Lauren who?
Lauren (law and) order.

Who's there?
Leif.
Leif who?
Leif me alone.

Who's there?
Lena.
Lena who?
Lena little closer. I have a secret to tell you.

Who's there?
Lilac.
Lilac who?
Lilac a trooper.

Who's there?
Lima bean.
Lima bean who?
"Lima bean (I've been) working on the railroad . . ."

Who's there?
Lion.
Lion who?
Lion down on the job again?

Who's there?
Lionel.
Lionel who?
Lionel bite you if you don't watch out.

Who's there?
Lisa.
Lisa who?
Lisa you can do is let me in.

Who's there?
Little old lady.
Little old lady who?
I didn't know you could yodel.

Who's there?
Livia.
Livia who?
Livia me alone!

Who's there?
Llama.
Llama who?
"Llama Yankee Doodle Dandy . . ."

Who's there?
Lois.
Lois who?
Lois man on the totem pole.

Who's there?
Louisiana.
Louisiana who?
Louisiana boy friend broke up.

Who's there?
Lucinda.
Lucinda who?
"Lucinda sky with diamonds . . ."

Who's there?
Lucretia.
Lucretia who?
Lucretia (the creature) from the Black Lagoon.

Who's there?
Luigi.
Luigi who?
Luigi board.

Who's there?
Luke.
Luke who?
Luke before you leap.

Who's there?
Lyndon.
Lyndon who?
Lyndon ear and I'll tell you.

KNOCK-KNOCK M

Who's there?
Madame.
Madame who?
Madame foot is caught in the door.

Who's there?
Major.
Major who?
Major answer this knock-knock joke.

Who's there?
Manuel.
Manuel who?
Manuel be sorry if you don't open this door.

Who's there?
Mara.
Mara who?
"Mara, Mara, on the wall . . ."

Who's there?
Marcella.
Marcella who?
Marcella is full of water and I'm drowning. Help!

Who's there?
Marion.
Marion who?
Marion haste, repent at leisure.

Who's there?
Marmalade.
Marmalade who?
"Marmalade (Momma laid) me," said the little chicken.

Who's there?
Matthew.
Matthew who?
Matthew is pinthing my foot.

Who's there?
Maura.
Maura who?
The Maura the merrier.

Who's there?
Max.
Max who?
Max no difference. Open the door.

Who's there?
Maybelle.
Maybelle who?
Maybelle (my bell) doesn't ring, either.

Who's there?
Meg.
Meg who?
Meg up your mind.

Who's there?
Melita.
Melita who?
Melita (my little) chickadee.

Who's there?
Meredith.
Meredith who?
Meredith (more of this) kind of knock-knock joke and I'm leaving.

Who's there?
Midas.
Midas who?
Midas well relax. I'm not going any place.

Who's there?
Minerva.
Minerva who?
Minerva-s wreck from all these questions.

Who's there?
Miniature.
Miniature who?
Miniature open your mouth,
you put your foot in it.

Who's there?
Minneapolis.
Minneapolis who?
Minneapolis each day keep
many doctors away.

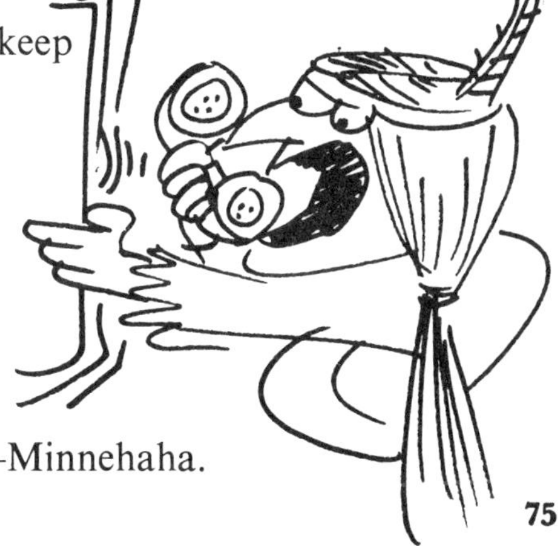

Who's there?
Minnie.
Minnie who?
No, not Minnie-who—Minnehaha.

KNOCK-KNOCK

Who's there?
Missouri.
Missouri who?
Missouri loves company.

Who's there?
Mitzi.
Mitzi who?
Mitzi door shut, you'll never find out.

Who's there?
Monkey.
Monkey who?
Monkey won't fit, that's why I knocked.

Who's there?
Moose.
Moose who?
Moose you be so nosy?

Who's there?
Morris.
Morris who?
Morris (tomorrow is) another day.

Who's there?
Mortimer.
Mortimer who?
Mortimer (more to her) than meets the eye.

Who's there?
Muffin.
Muffin who?
Muffin grouchy in the morning.

Who's there?
Myth.
Myth who?
Myth you, too.

KNOCK-KNOCK

Who's there?
Nadya.
Nadya who?
Nadya head if you
understand what I'm saying.

Who's there?
Nana.
Nana who?
Nana your business.

Who's there?
Nettie.
Nettie who?
Nettie as a fruitcake.

Who's there?
Noah.
Noah who?
"Noahbody knows the trouble I've seen . . ."

Who's there?
Norma Lee.
Norma Lee who?
Norma Lee I don't go around knocking on doors, but I have this wonderful set of encyclopedias . . .

Who's there?
Nuisance.
Nuisance who?
What's nuisance yesterday?

Who's there?
Nurse.
Nurse who?
Nurse sense in talking to you.

KNOCK-KNOCK

Who's there?
Obadiah. (Pronounced O-bad-eye-ah)
Obadiah who?
Obadiah (oh, I'm dying) from dis cold.

Who's there?
Ocelot.
Ocelot who?
Ocelot of questions, don't you?

Who's there?
Odette.
Odette who?
Odette's a bad sign.

Who's there?
Odessa.
Odessa who?
Odessa hot one!

Who's there?
Odysseus. (Pronounced Oh-diss-us)
Odysseus who?
Odysseus the last straw!

Who's there?
Ogre.
Ogre who?
Ogre take a flying leap!

Who's there?
Ohio.
Ohio who?
Ohio feeling?
Knock-Knock.
Who's there?
Kentucky.
Kentucky who?
Kentucky (can't talk) too well, have a sore throat.
Knock-Knock.
Who's there?
Nevada.
Nevada who?
Nevada saw you look worse.
You should be in bed.

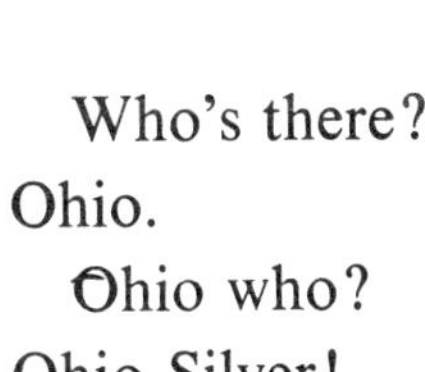

Who's there?
Ohio.
Ohio who?
Ohio Silver!

knock-knock

Who's there?
Olaf.
Olaf who?
Olaf you.

Who's there?
Oldest son.
Oldest son who?
"Oldest son shines bright on my old Kentucky home . . ."

Who's there?
Olga.
Olga who?
Olga way when I'm good and ready.

Who's there?
Olive.
Olive who?
Olive none of your lip.

Who's there?
Oliver.
Oliver who?
Oliver troubles are over.

Who's there?
Olivia.
Olivia who?
Olivia (I live here) but I forgot my key.

Who's there?
Ollie.
Ollie who?
Ollie time you say that, I wish you'd cut it out.

Who's there?
Omar.
Omar who?
Omar goodness gracious! Wrong door!

Who's there?
Omega.
Omega who?
Omega best man win!

Who's there?
Ooze.
Ooze who?
Ooze in charge around here?

KNOCK-KNOCK

Who's there?
Opera.
Opera who?
Opera-tunity. And you thought opportunity only knocked once!

Who's there?
Orange juice.
Orange juice who?
Orange juice going to talk to me?

Who's there?
Orson.
Orson who?
Orson around again?

Who's there?
Orson.
Orson who?
Orson buggy is about your speed.

Who's there?
Osborn.
Osborn who?
Osborn today—it's my birthday!

Who's there?
Oscar.
Oscar who?
Oscar silly question,
get a silly answer.

Who's there?
O'Shea.
O'Shea who?
O'Shea, that's a
shad shtory.

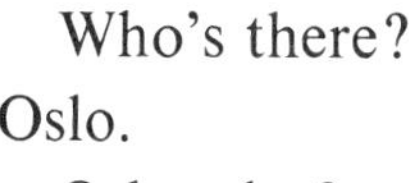

Who's there?
Oslo.
Oslo who?
Oslo down. Where's the fire?

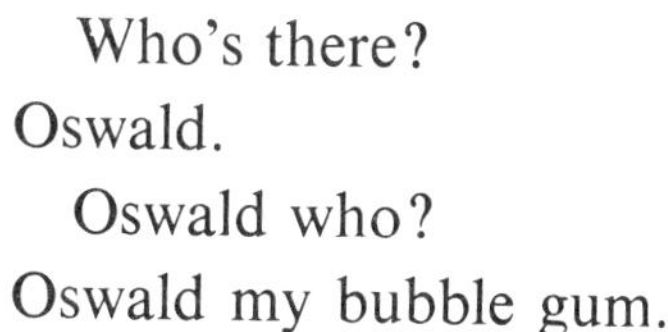

Who's there?
Oswald.
Oswald who?
Oswald my bubble gum.

Who's there?
Oswego.
Oswego who?
"Oswego marching, marching home . . ."

Who's there?
Othello. (Pronounced Oh-thell-oh)
Othello who?
Othello you thalked to me.

Knock-Knock

Who's there?
Ottawa.
Ottawa who?
Ottawa know you're telling the truth?

Knock-Knock.
Who's there?
Otis.
Otis who?
Otis a sin to tell a lie.

Who's there?
Owen.
Owen who?
Owen (oh, when) you open this door,
I'm going to give you such a hit . . .

Who's there?
Owl.
Owl who?
Owl aboard!

Who's there?
Ozzie.
Ozzie who?
Ozzie you later.

P

Who's there?
Pajamas.
Pajamas who?
"Pajamas (Put your arms a-) 'round me, honey, hold me tight . . ."

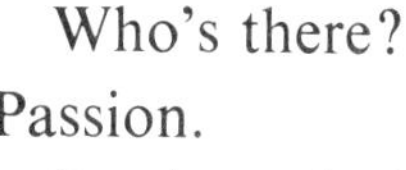

Who's there?
Passion.
Passion who?
Passion by and thought I'd say "Hello."

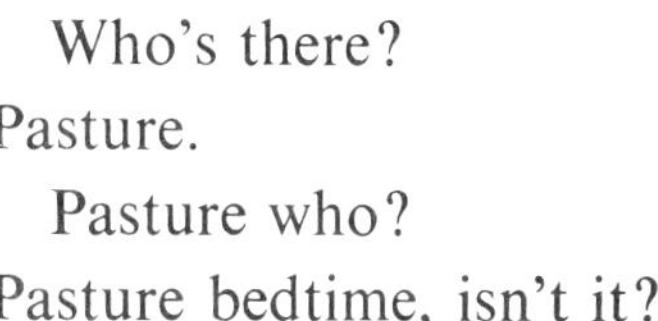

Who's there?
Pasture.
Pasture who?
Pasture bedtime, isn't it?

Who's there?
Pecan.
Pecan who?
Pecan (pick on) somebody your own size!

KNOCK-KNOCK

Who's there?
Pharaoh.
Pharaoh who?
Pharaoh 'nuff.

Who's there?
Phineas. (Pronounced Finny-us)
Phineas who?
Phineas thing happened on the way to the forum . . .

Who's there?
Philippa.
Philippa who?
Philippa bathtub. I'm dirty.

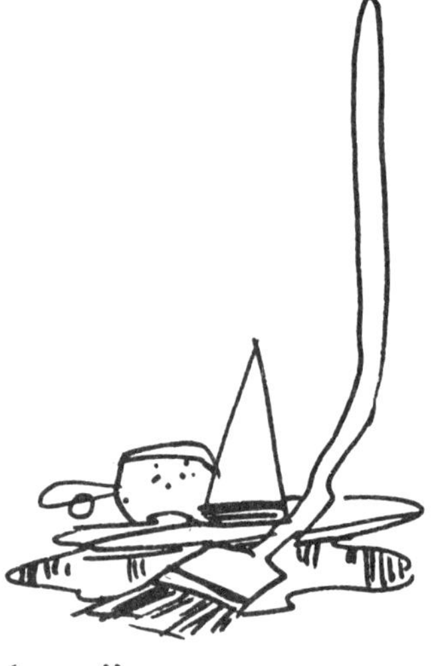

Who's there?
Phyllis.
Phyllis who?
Phyllis in on the news.

Who's there?
Ping pong.
Ping pong who?
"Ping pong, the witch is dead . . ."

Who's there?
Plato.
Plato who?
Plato spaghetti and meatballs, please.

Who's there?
Police.
Police who?
Police open the door.

Who's there?
Possum.
Possum who?
Possum peace pipe.

Who's there?
Punch.
Punch who?
Not me—I just got here!

knock knock

Who's there?
Quacker.
Quacker who?
Quacker 'nother bad joke and I'm leaving.

Who's there?
Quebec.
Quebec who?
Quebec to the end of the line.

Who's there?
Quiet Tina.
Quiet Tina who?
Quiet Tina courtroom—monkey wants to speak.

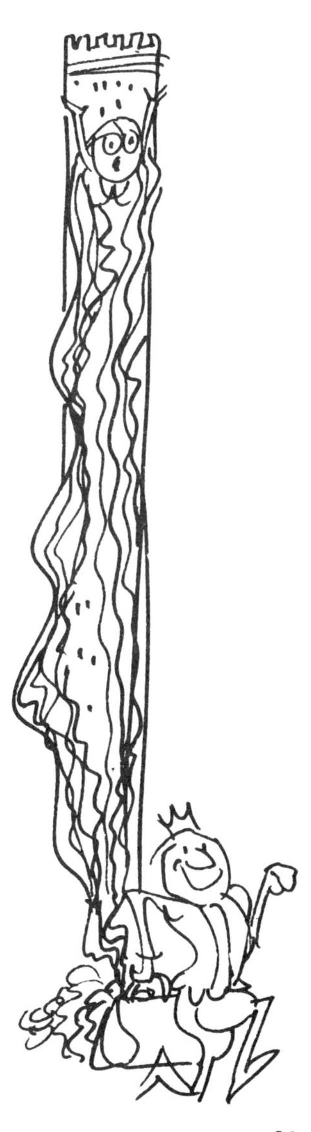

Who's there?
Rabbit.
Rabbit who?
Rabbit up neatly. It's a present.

Who's there?
Raleigh.
Raleigh who?
Raleigh round the flag, boys.

Who's there?
Rapunzel.
Rapunzel who?
"Rapunzel troubles in
your old kit bag and
smile, smile, smile . . ."

Who's there?
Razor.
Razor who?
Razor hands—this is a stick-up!

KNOCK-KNOCK

Who's there?
Red.
Red who?
Red peppers. Isn't that a hot one?

Who's there?
Rhoda.
Rhoda who?
"Row, row, Rhoda boat . . ."

Who's there?
Robin.
Robin who?
Robin the piggy bank again?

Who's there?
Rocky.
Rocky who?
"Rocky bye baby
on the tree top . . ."

Who's there?
Roland.
Roland who?
Roland stone gathers no moss.

Who's there?
Rona.
Rona who?
Rona the mill.

Who's there?
Roxanne.
Roxanne who?
Roxanne your head or something?

Who's there?
Rufus.
Rufus who?
Rufus leaking and I'm getting wet.

KNOCK-KNOCK

S

Who's there?
Sabina.
Sabina who?
Sabina long time since I've seen you.

Knock-Knock.
Who's there?
Mischa.
Mischa who?
Mischa a lot.

Who's there?
Sacha.
Sacha who?
Sacha fuss, just because I knocked at your door.

Who's there?
Sadie.
Sadie who?
Sadie Pledge of Allegiance.

Who's there?
Safari.
Safari who?
Safari so good.

Who's there?
Sam and Janet.
Sam and Janet who?
"Sam and Janet evening, you will meet a stranger . . ."

Who's there?
Sarah.
Sarah who?
Sarah doctor in the house?

KNOCK-KNOCK

Who's there?
Saul.
Saul who?
"Saul the King's horses and Saul the King's men . . ."

Who's there?
Savannah.
Savannah who?
Savannah you going to open the door?

Who's there?
Says.
Says who?
Says me, that's who!

Who's there?
Schachter.
Schachter who?
Schachter Ripper. Feel like cutting up?

Who's there?
Schatzi.
Schatzi who?
Schatzi way the ball bounces.

Who's there?
Scissor.
Scissor who?
Scissor and Cleopatra.

Who's there?
Scold.
Scold who?
Scold outside.

Who's there?
Seymour.
Seymour who?
Seymour if you'd get the door open.

Who's there?
Sharon.
Sharon who?
Sharon share alike.

Who's there?
Sheila.
Sheila who?
"Sheila be coming round the mountain when she comes . . ."

knock-knock

Who's there?
Shelly Cohn.
Shelly Cohn who?
Shelly Cohn (chili con) carne.

Who's there?
Sherry.
Sherry who?
Sherry dance?

Who's there?
Sherwood.
Sherwood who?
Sherwood like to help you out;
which way did you come in?

Who's there?
Shirley.
Shirley who?
Shirley you must know me by now.

Who's there?
Sicily.
Sicily who?
Sicily question.

Who's there?
Sinbad.
Sinbad who?
Sinbad and you'll never get to heaven.

Who's there?
Sizzle.
Sizzle who?
Sizzle hurt me more than it hurts you.

Who's there?
Soda.
Soda who?
Soda you!

Who's there?
Sonata.
Sonata who?
Sonata such a big deal.

KNOCK-KNOCK

Who's there?
Sonia.
Sonia who?
"Sonia paper moon . . ."

Who's there?
Spider.
Spider who?
Spider what everyone says, I like you.

Who's there?
Stan.
Stan who?
Stan back, I'm going to sneeze!

Who's there?
Stanton.
Stanton who?
Stanton here answering questions is no fun.

Who's there?
Statue.
Statue who?
Statue? This is me.

Who's there?
Stefan.
Stefan who?
Stefan it quick before it reproduces!

Who's there?
Stepfather.
Stepfather who?
One stepfather (step farther) and I'll let you have it.

Who's there?
Stopwatch.
Stopwatch who?
Stopwatch you're doing this minute!

Who's there?
Stu.
Stu who?
Stu late to ask questions.

Who's there?
Sultan.
Sultan who?
Sultan pepper.

KNOCK-KNOCK

Who's there?
Summertime.
Summertime who?
Summertime you can be a big pest.

Who's there?
Sybil.
Sybil who?
Sybil Simon met a pieman . . .

Who's there?
Tad.
Tad who?
Tad-s all, folks!

Who's there?
Tamara.
Tamara who?
Tamara the world.

Who's there?
Tank.
Tank who?
You're welcome.
Knock-Knock.
Who's there?
Dimension.
Dimension who?
Dimension it.

Knock-Knock

Who's there?
Tarzan.
Tarzan who?
Tarzan stripes forever.

Who's there?
Teachers.
Teachers who?
Teachers (three cheers) for the red, white and blue!

Who's there?
Tennis.
Tennis who?
Tennis five plus five.

Who's there?
Tex.
Tex who?
Tex two to tango.

Who's there?
Thatcher.
Thatcher who?
Thatcher could get away with it.

Who's there?
Thayer.
Thayer who?
Thayer thorry and I won't throw this pie in your face.

Who's there?
Thea.
Thea who?
Thea later, alligator.

Who's there?
Thelonius.
Thelonius who?
Thelonius kid in town.

Who's there?
Theodore.
Theodore who?
Theodore is closed, open up!

Who's there?
Theresa.
Theresa who?
Theresa fly in my soup.

KNOCK-KNOCK

Who's there?
Therese.
Therese who?
Therese many a slip twixt the cup and the lip.

Who's there?
Thermos.
Thermos who?
Thermos be a better way.

Who's there?
Thumb.
Thumb who?
Thumb like it hot and thumb like it cold.

Who's there?
Thumping.
Thumping who?
Thumping green and slimy is climbing up your neck.

Who's there?
Tibet.
Tibet who?
Early Tibet and early to rise .

Who's there?
Tinker Bell.
Tinker Bell who?
Tinker Bell is out of order.

Who's there?
Toby.
Toby who?
Toby or not Toby.
Knock-Knock.
Who's there?
Thaddeus.
Thaddeus who?
Thaddeus question.

Who's there?
Tom Sawyer.
Tom Sawyer who?
Tom Sawyer underwear.
Knock-Knock.
Who's there?
Arkansas.
Arkansas who?
Arkansas it, too!

Knock-knock

Who's there?
Toothy.
Toothy who?
Toothy, the day after Monday.

Who's there?
Torch.
Torch who?
Torch you would never ask.

Who's there?
Toucan.
Toucan who?
Toucan live as cheaply as one.

Who's there?
Toyota.
Toyota who?
Toyota be a law against knock-knock jokes.

Who's there?
Tuna.
Tuna who?
Tuna your radio down, you're making too much noise.

Who's there?
Turnip.
Turnip who?
Turnip the heat.
It's cold out here.

Who's there?
Twig.
Twig who?
Twig or tweet!

Who's there?
Typhoid.
Typhoid who?
Typhoid that song before.

Who's there?
Tyrone.
Tyrone who?
Tyrone shoe laces. You're big enough now.

KNOCK-KNOCK

U

Who's there?
Uganda.
Uganda who?
Uganda get away with this.

Who's there?
Uriah.
Uriah who?
Keep Uriah on the ball.

Who's there?
Uruguay.
Uruguay who?
You go Uruguay and I'll go mine.

Who's there?
Usher.
Usher who?
Usher wish you would let me in.

Who's there?
Uta.
Uta who?
Uta sight, uta mind.

Who's there?
Utica.
Utica who?
Utica high road and I'll take the low road.

KNOCK-KNOCK

Who's there?
Valencia. (Pronounced Va-len-see-ya)
Valencia who?
Valencia dollar, will you pay it back?

Who's there?
Value.
Value who?
Value be my Valentine?

Who's there?
Vanessa.
Vanessa who?
Vanessa you going to grow up?

Who's there?
Vanilla.
Vanilla who?
Vanilla call the doctor.

Who's there?
Vassar girl.
Vassar girl who?
Vassar girl like you doing in a place like this?

Who's there?
Vaughan.
Vaughan who?
"Vaughan day my prince will come . . ."

Who's there?
Veal chop.
Veal chop who?
Veal chop for a used car.

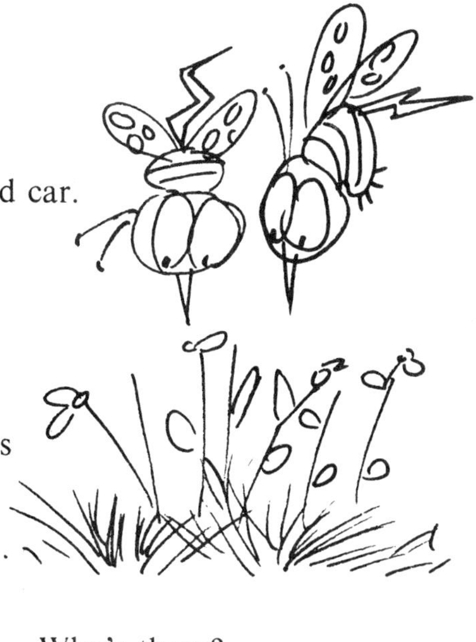

Who's there?
Vera.
Vera who?
"Vera all the flowers gone . . ."

Who's there?
Viola.
Viola who?
Viola sudden you don't know me?

KNOCK-KNOCK

Who's there?
Violet.
Violet who?
Violet the cat out of the bag?

Who's there?
Virtue.
Virtue who?
Virtue get those big, brown eyes?

Who's there?
Viscount. (Pronounced V-eye-count)
Viscount who?
Viscount you behave?

Who's there?
Voodoo.
Voodoo who?
Voodoo you think you are, the Wolf Man?

Who's there?
Waddle.
Waddle who?
Waddle you give me if I go away?

Who's there?
Wafer.
Wafer who?
Wafer a long time,
but here I am again.

Who's there?
Wah.
Wah who?
Well, you don't have to
get so excited about it!

Who's there?
Waiter.
Waiter who?
Waiter I get my hands on you!

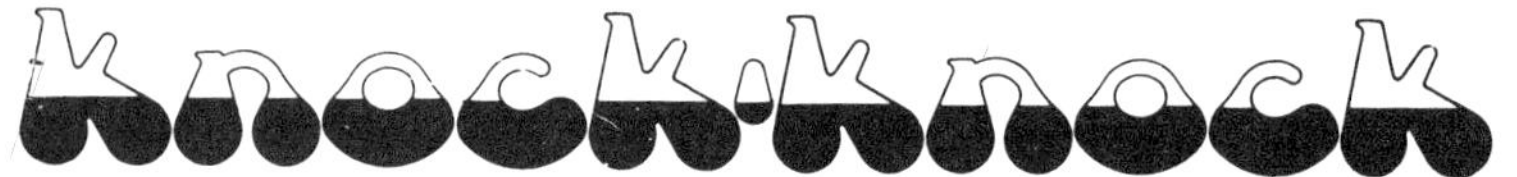

Who's there?
Wallace.
Wallace who?
Wallace (we all are) saying nasty things about you.

Who's there?
Walnuts.
Walnuts who?
Walnuts around here.

Who's there?
Walter.
Walter who?
Walter-wall carpeting.

Who's there?
Wanda.
Wanda who?
Wanda buy some Girl Scout cookies?

Who's there?
Wannetta.
Wannetta who?
Wannetta time, please.

Who's there?
Warner.
Warner who?
Warner you coming out to play?

Who's there?
Warren.
Warren who?
Warren my birthday suit.

Who's there?
Warrior.
Warrior who?
Warrior been all my life?

Who's there?
Wash.
Wash who?
Wash you there, Charlie?

Who's there?
Water.
Water who?
Water be ashamed of yourself
for living in a dump like this!

KNOCK-KNOCK

Who's there?
Water skier.
Water skier who?
Water skier'd of? I'm harmless.

Who's there?
Watson.
Watson who?
Watson your mind?

Who's there?
Watusi.
Watusi who?
Watusi is what you get.

Who's there?
Wayne.
Wayne who?
Wayne are you coming over to my house?

Who's there?
Weevil.
Weevil who?
Weevil work it out.

Who's there?
Weirdo.
Weirdo who?
Weirdo you think you're going?

Who's there?
Welcome.
Welcome who?
Welcome up and
see me sometime.

Who's there?
Wendy.
Wendy who?
"Wendy wind blows,
the cradle will rock . . ."

Who's there?
Wheelbarrow.
Wheelbarrow who?
Wheelbarrow some money and go on a trip.

Who's there?
Whitney.
Whitney who?
Whitney have to say to me?

KNOCK-KNOCK

Who's there?
Whittle.
Whittle who?
Whittle Orphan Annie.

Who's there?
Who.
Who who?
You sound like an owl.

Who's there?
Wicked..
Wicked who?
Wicked make beautiful music together.

Who's there?
Will you remember me in a week?
Yes.
Will you remember me in a month?
Yes.
Will you remember me in a year?
Yes.
Will you remember me in five years?
Yes.
Knock-Knock.
Who's there?
See! You've forgotten me already.

Who's there?
Willis.
Willis who?
Willis rain ever stop?

Who's there?
Willoughby.
Willoughby who?
Willoughby a monkey's uncle!

Who's there?
Wilma.
Wilma who?
Wilma dreams come true?

Who's there?
Wooden shoe.
Wooden shoe who?
Wooden shoe like to know?

KNOCK-KNOCK

Who's there?
X.
X who?
X for breakfast.

Who's there?
Xavier.
Xavier who?
Xavier breath! I'm not leaving.

Who's there?
Xenia.
Xenia who?
Xenia stealing my *Mad Magazine*.

Who's there?
Yacht.
Yacht who?
Yacht 'a know me by now.

Who's there?
Yachts.
Yachts who?
Yachts up, Doc?

Who's there?
Yah.
Yah who?
Ride 'em, cowboy!

KNOCK·KNOCK

Who's there?
Yelp.
Yelp who?
Yelp me—My nose is stuck in the keyhole.

Who's there?
Yoga.
Yoga who?
Yoga what it takes!

Who's there?
Yogi Bear.
Yogi Bear who?
Yogi Bear (you go bare) and you're going to get arrested.

Who's there?
Yolanda.
Yolanda who?
Yolanda me some money?

Who's there?
You.
You who?
You who yourself!

Who's there?
Yucatan.
Yucatan who?
"Yucatan fool some
of the people
some of the time . . ."

Who's there?
Yucca.
Yucca who?
Yucca catch more
flies with honey
than with vinegar.

Who's there?
Yukon.
Yukon who?
Yukon say that again.

Who's there?
Yvonne.
Yvonne who?
Yvonne to be alone?

Knock-Knock

Z

Who's there?
Zany.
Zany who?
Zany body home?

Who's there?
Zeke.
Zeke who?
"Zeke and ye shall find . . ."

Who's there?
Zinnia.
Zinnia who?
Zinnia on TV—do you really have fewer cavities?

Who's there?
Zippy.
Zippy who?
Mrs. Zippy.

Who's there?
Zizi.
Zizi who?
Zizi when you know how.

Who's there?
Zone.
Zone who?
Zone shadow scares him.

Who's there?
Zookeeper.
Zookeeper who?
Zookeeper way from me!

Who's there?
Zoom.
Zoom who?
Zoom did you expect?

Who's there?
Zsa Zsa.
Zsa Zsa who?
Zsa Zsa last knock-knock joke I want to hear.

Index of Subjects & Hidden Names

Some names are not listed alphabetically in this dictionary. Check this index if you don't see them.